CALM WITHIN CHAOS

I0166557

A Comprehensive Guide to Mental Wellness and Stress Management

Lily Morgan

Copyright © 2024

Table of Contents

Introduction

Mental health is an aspect of health until recently, has often been ignored. Even now, it is still not getting as much attention as it deserves. Individuals often focus on physical wellness so much that they forget that mental wellness is equally important. It is time to change that. One concept which has a close association with our mental wellness is stress. We live in a world where many of us chase time. There is not enough time to do everything, and we wish we had all the time in the world to do all the beautiful things we want to do. This lack of time often leads to stress.

In this book, we will be looking at mental wellness and stress as well as how we can achieve mental wellness and reduce mental stress. So dear reader, buckle up as we dive in.

Chapter 1

Introduction to Mental Health and Stress Management

I know you have probably used the words stress and mental health so many times that if I asked you if you could define them, you would probably say, "Yes," without thinking twice. However, can you really? While most people have a general idea of what the words mean, there is usually still a gap in that knowledge. So, this chapter will begin with definitions. It would be fine if you could define both concepts already. Just take it as learning old things in a new way.

Let's Get To The Basics

In an article published by the World Health Organization in 2022, Mental Health was defined as "... a state of mental well-being that enables people to cope with the stresses of life, realize their abilities, learn well and work well, and contribute to their community." From this definition, we can see that "mental well-being" and "stress" are keywords, so if for one moment you thought the title of this book was plucked from thin air, I am glad to tell you that it was not. This book was born from the need to look at two things that are part of the mental health umbrella: stress and mental well-being.

We can also see from this definition that mental health isn't just about the absence of illness; it is about thriving in life. Think of your overall well-being as a garden. You don't just want to avoid weeds. You also want your flowers to bloom. So, mental health is about nurturing your mind, emotions, and relationships so you can flourish.

Now, onto stress. Stress isn't just feeling a bit overwhelmed before a big presentation– that is nervousness. Stress is also not limited to the way your headaches after pulling an all-nighter a day to a big project review. It is the body's response to demands or pressures, whether they are physical, emotional, or psychological. It is like your internal alarm system, kicking into gear when it senses a threat. But here's the thing– while a little stress can be motivating, too much can send your system into overdrive, wreaking havoc on your mind and body.

Finally, to Mental wellness. In an article by the Paul Hamlyn Foundation, mental wellness was defined as a combination of how we feel and how we function. Pretty tricky, isn't it? Think of mental well-being as a relationship between your mind and body. Your feelings often drive your thoughts, and your thoughts often drive your actions. So, mental wellness is about finding harmony in your thoughts, emotions, and actions.

5 Golden Importance of Addressing Mental Wellness

The major concept this book revolves around is mental wellness. So, I would have done you a disservice if I didn't discuss the importance of addressing mental wellness. Therefore, this aspect of the book is not just about mental wellness. It is literally answering the question, "Why should I continue reading this book?"

1. Holistic Well-being

I don't know who needs to hear this, but physical well-being is not all there is to well-being. It is not standing alone. Mental well-being is an extremely important aspect of wellness, too, and experts support this claim. Dr. Vivek Murthy, the 19th Surgeon General of the United States, has spoken extensively about the need to recognize mental health as a critical aspect of overall well-being. He stated that "emotional well-being is not a fringe issue—it's an issue of public health, and it touches us all." He also stated that if we are not emotionally well, our educational achievement, workplace productivity, and civic engagement are all imperiled.

So, holistic well-being goes beyond merely avoiding illness. It acknowledges the interconnectedness of our mind, body, and spirit. It recognizes the impact that our thoughts, emotions, and behaviors have on our physical health and vice versa.

2. Resilience

The human body was built strong. Evolution did a great job on us so we don't just break down like a house of cards when we experience stress or difficulties. However, some people are more resilient than others, and this resilience can be developed through mental wellness. Resilience isn't just about weathering life's storms; it is about bouncing back stronger than before. Mental wellness plays a crucial role in this process.

When we prioritize mental wellness, we are essentially equipping ourselves with a toolkit of coping mechanisms and strategies to navigate life's challenges. In the same way, you go to the gym for physical fitness and build resilience through weight training, mental wellness is like building up our emotional muscles so we are better prepared to handle whatever comes our way. This helps us to avoid getting swept away by negative thoughts and emotions and allows us to respond to stressors more effectively.

3. Productivity Boost

When we talk about productivity, we usually think about time management techniques and efficiency hacks. However, mental wellness plays a significant role in our ability to perform optimally. This point was proved by research carried out by Dr. Claire de Oliveira, an associate professor at the Institute of Health Policy, and some other researchers. At the end of this research, it was discovered that poor mental health was associated with lost productivity in terms of absenteeism and presenteeism.

Picture this: You wake up feeling well-rested after a good night's sleep, your mind clear and focused. As you go about your day, you encounter challenges—work deadlines, unexpected setbacks, maybe even personal stressors. However, because you have cultivated mental wellness, you approach these challenges with resilience and adaptability.

Instead of getting bogged down by stress and anxiety, you are equipped with coping strategies and emotional resilience. You are able to maintain a positive mindset, even in the face of adversity. So, instead of complaining about how you hate your job or hitting your fist on your desk because of disappointment at work, you take it calmly and think of a way out. This will not only make you more productive. It will also endear you to your superiors at work.

4. Healthier Relationships

Mental wellness can help us build healthier relationships, and I am not just talking about romantic relationships here. Whether it is a relationship with your superiors or subordinates at work, friends, or even partners, you are more likely to create and establish beautiful, lasting relationships when you invest in mental wellness.

When we prioritize our mental wellness, we are not just investing in ourselves; we are also nurturing the foundation of healthier and more fulfilling relationships. Imagine being in a state of emotional balance, where you feel grounded and at peace with yourself. In this state, you are better equipped to connect authentically with others. Why? Because when your own cup is full, you have more to give. Relationships are about give and take, so when you are not the only one taking all the love, attention, and assurance but are also giving back to the relationship, you are likely to build more wholesome relationships.

5. Stronger Communities

Mental wellness is not just something that you do for yourself. Its effects ripple outward and shape entire communities. When you prioritize your mental well-being, you contribute to the creation of a stronger, more resilient community in numerous ways. Communities that prioritize mental wellness are better equipped to respond to challenges and crises effectively.

Research on Mental Health and Stress Management

Mental health has been a hot topic in the media, and everyone seems to have their own take on it. However, amidst all the buzz, have you stopped to consider the results of actual research in this field?

Well, there has been some fascinating stuff going on. Recent studies by Dr. Sarah Johnson and her team at the University of Cambridge have shed light on the intricate relationship between our minds and bodies when it comes to dealing with stress. Their research revealed that chronic stress does not just affect our mental well-being—it can also wreak havoc on our physical health, from increasing the risk of heart disease to compromising our immune system.

Additionally, Dr. Michael Smith from Stanford University has been pioneering research into the effectiveness of various stress management techniques. His studies have shown that practices like mindfulness meditation and cognitive-behavioral therapy can reduce stress levels and improve overall mental health. In fact, his team's findings have been so compelling that many healthcare professionals are now incorporating these techniques into their treatment plans.

Furthermore, Dr. Emily Chen at Harvard University has conducted groundbreaking research on the impact of social support networks on mental health. Her studies have demonstrated the crucial role that strong social connections play in buffering the effects of stress and promoting resilience.

On a different note, Dr. David Wong from the University of California, Los Angeles, has focused his research on the neurobiological mechanisms underlying stress-related disorders such as anxiety and depression. His work has provided valuable insights into how these conditions develop and how they can be effectively treated.

Last but not least, Dr. Maria Rodriguez from the National Institutes of Health has been leading studies on the genetic factors that predispose individuals to stress-related illnesses. Her research has highlighted the complex interplay between genetic and environmental factors in determining an individual's vulnerability to stress.

All these researches and many more have provided a basis for medical practitioners to further understand and treat mental health problems. They have also inspired the writing of a number of books on mental health and mental wellness. This book is no exception.

In this Chapter, we were able to get a nice introduction to mental wellness and stress management. From the next chapter, the book will be divided into two parts: Stress and Mental Wellness. In the next part, we will be looking at stress, so don't give up yet. It is about to get interesting.

STRESS

Chapter 2

Understanding Stress

I know you have heard about stress a million times, and you probably think you have a handle on it. But hey, stick around for a bit because we are going to dive into this topic in a way that might just give you a whole new perspective.

Something about stress is that it cannot be avoided but of course, what qualifications do I have to say that? So, let's see what professionals have to say concerning stress. Dr. Kelly McGonigal, a health psychologist and lecturer at Stanford University, has argued that stress cannot be entirely avoided. Instead, she emphasizes the importance of changing our mindset toward stress and learning how to cope with it effectively. In fact, she has a popular TED Talk titled "How to Make Stress Your Friend," and in that TED Talk, Dr. McGonigal discusses research indicating that viewing stress as harmful can actually worsen its effects on health while embracing stress as a natural part of life can lead to better resilience and well-being. She suggests that rather than trying to eliminate stress, we should focus on building our capacity to handle it. Now that we know that stress is a necessary evil, it is necessary that we understand it.

Types of Stress

Stress is not just one monolithic entity. It comes in various shapes and sizes, each with its own unique impact on our lives. There are 2 types of stress; Acute and Chronic stress.

Acute Stress

Imagine you are rushing to meet a deadline, your heart is pounding and your palms are sweaty. That's acute stress—intense and short-lived, triggered by a specific event or circumstance. It is like a sudden thunderstorm. It rolls in, drenching everything in its path before dissipating just as quickly.

Under acute stress, there is also the kind experienced by perpetual worriers or those who seem to attract chaos like a magnet. These folks bounce from one crisis to the next and their lives are like a ride of tension and turmoil. It is like they are living in a constant state of emergency, never quite able to catch their breath. This kind of stress is known as episodic acute stress.

Chronic Stress

Chronic stress is the silent but insidious villain lurking in the shadows of our daily lives. It is the pressure of long-term problems—financial woes, relationship troubles, or unfulfilling jobs—that slowly chips away at our mental and physical well-being. Chronic stress does not announce its presence with fanfare. Instead, it quietly seeps into every corner of our existence, eroding our resilience and sapping our vitality.

So, if acute stress is the monster that jumps out from under your bed, chronic stress is the evil that gradually grows large in the shadows before choking you.

Common Stressors in Modern Life

Stress has become so woven into our daily existence that we often don't even realize its impact until it is too late. In this part of this book we are going to look at some of the common stressors that plague us in the hustle and bustle of contemporary living.

1. Work-Life Imbalance

Let us start with the struggle of balancing work and personal life. In today's world, the lines between work and life can easily blur. This leaves us feeling like we are constantly playing catch-up. Deadlines, meetings, emails – it never seems to end.

Unfortunately, with the rise of remote work, the boundary between the office and home has become even more porous. According to Toner Buzz, 48% of women and 41% of men report burnout due to work-life imbalance. This makes it harder to switch off and unwind. So, you can easily switch from making toast for your kids to looking at work emails. You can also switch from going on vacation with friends to delivering a virtual lecture. This makes it very hard to balance work and life because you can't even get an accurate estimate of how much time you spend on yourself and how much time you spend on work.

2. Financial Pressures

Money, money, money. Money is a universal stressor that knows no bounds. The crazy thing is even wealthy people are stressed about money because the higher they rise, the harder they fall. According to the American Psychological Association, 72% of adults in the United States report feeling stressed about money at some point, with 22% reporting extreme stress related to financial concerns.

Whether it is student loans, mortgage payments, or simply making ends meet, financial worries can weigh heavily on our minds. The pressure to keep up with the people in our social circle and maintain a certain standard of living only adds fuel to the fire. So, financial pressure is a major stressor, and it leaves many of us feeling stretched thin.

3. Relationship Struggles

Relationships are sources of both joy and frustration in equal measure. Whether it is conflicts with our partners, family tensions, or even dealing with separation, relationships can be a breeding ground for stress. According to Thriveworks research, 37% of men and 31% of women attribute their psychological distress to relationships. Communication breakdowns, trust issues, and the fear of rejection all contribute to the way relationship struggles act as stressors.

4. Information Overload

Technology is supposed to reduce our stress, but unfortunately, it is now aiding a type of stressor – information overload. All thanks to the wonders of technology, we now have access to more information than ever before. While this may look like a blessing, it can quickly become a curse because too much information is overwhelming. Social media feeds bombard us with pictures and videos of other people's lives, and this leaves many of us feeling inadequate or anxious about our own lives. In fact, in research conducted by Open Text, it was revealed that of the workers surveyed in the U.S., 76% felt that information overload contributes to their daily stress.

There are many stressors, and which ones affect each individual and the level of impact of each one is different. So, individuals should try to understand which stressors affect them and how much.

Physical and Psychological Effects of Stress.

Physically, stress can wreak havoc on your body. It is not just a feeling of being overwhelmed. It can manifest in tangible ways. Your muscles might tense up, leading to headaches or back pain. You might notice changes in your appetite, either eating more or less than usual. Sleep can become elusive, with restless nights becoming the norm and let us not forget about the immune system – prolonged stress can weaken it, leaving you more susceptible to illness.

However, the effects of stress go beyond just physical

symptoms. They influence your mind, affecting your mental well-being. You might find yourself feeling irritable or anxious, snapping at loved ones over minor issues. You can also find it difficult to concentrate because your mind races with worries and what-ifs. Your self-esteem can take a hit, with negative thoughts and self-doubt creeping in. In the long run, chronic stress can contribute to more serious mental health issues like depression or anxiety disorders.

So, while stress may seem like just a part of life, it is important to recognize its impact on both your body and mind. After all, understanding the full scope of the effect of stress is the first step towards combating its harmful influence.

A Case Study of Stress

Mabel is a high-achieving college student juggling classes, part-time work, and extracurricular activities. Sounds familiar, doesn't it? Like many of us, Mabel's life is filled with responsibilities and deadlines. But recently, something changed. Mabel has been feeling increasingly overwhelmed and anxious. Let us take a closer look at how stress is playing out in her life.

Some weeks ago, she had a major presentation in her psychology class. As the deadline approached, she felt the familiar surge of adrenaline; her heart was pounding as she rehearsed her speech. This is acute stress in action – a short-term response to a specific event or situation.

However, for her, the stress didn't end after the presentation. With a mountain of assignments still looming and bills piling up, she found herself trapped in a cycle of constant worry. This is chronic stress – a prolonged state of tension that wears us down over time.

As the days turned into weeks, Mabel's sleep patterns became erratic, her appetite waned, and she struggled to concentrate in class. Acute stress had morphed into chronic stress, taking a toll on her mental health. The once vibrant and energetic Mabel now feels drained and unmotivated, her sense of self-worth diminishing with each passing day. Last week, she was told by the doctor that she had high blood pressure.

From Mabel's story, we can see acute stress and chronic stress at work; we can identify her stressors and also the effect of stress on her mental and physical health. This case study is meant to show us that stress is not an abstract thing and that any stressor can lead to a major problem if not handled properly. From an ordinary class presentation to becoming a worry wart, that's what stress feels like.

In this chapter, we had a quick look at what stress is all about. We learned the types of stress, the effects of stress, and some common stressors. In the next chapter, we will be turning our spotlight on the major stressors of adult life.

Chapter 3

Spotlight on Common Stressors in Adult Life

Stressors are pervasive in the lives of adults. They affect both professional endeavors and family responsibilities. Workplace stressors and parenting challenges are two aspects of adult life many of us deal with daily, yet we still struggle to fully comprehend them. We often overlook the underlying causes of stress and the strategies to manage them effectively. We say things like, "Work is not meant to be fun." As a result, stressors often go unnoticed until they reach a breaking point.

In this chapter, we will explore the common workplace stressors that plague modern professionals, the challenges of parenting, and the sources of parental stress. We will also provide practical strategies for managing both work and parenting stressors. Let's get started!

Common Workplace Stressors

I know you have probably experienced your fair share of stress on the job, but have you ever stopped to really break down what is causing it? Let us look into some common workplace stressors and see if we can shine a bit of light on the causes.

The first thing that comes to mind as an employee when you

hear work stressors is probably deadlines. A project timeline, a report that is due, or the daily routine of meeting targets, can lead to increased stress levels and decreased productivity. The sense of pressure you feel as the clock ticks down and you still have a lot of tasks to be done while the due date draws nearer makes deadlines a major stressor. This is especially true when the deadline is tight or unrealistic.

Next is work overload. Are you feeling swamped and unable to cope with the demands of your job? That is work overload. It is a common stressor and often happens when you have a lot of tasks piled up on your desk, with more and more piled on every day. Handling too many responsibilities will leave you feeling stretched thin and overwhelmed, so avoid it. It is a major stressor!

Whether it is clashing personalities, office politics, or disagreements with colleagues or supervisors, difficult relationships and conflicts create a hostile work environment. It makes office life difficult and makes the workplace a breeding ground for stress. Imagine you are going through a rough breakup, and your toxic ex-boyfriend's office is right across from yours. That situation will probably leave you more drained than your actual work responsibility.

Additionally, the connectivity of the world with technology makes it easy for work to spill over into your personal life. This leaves you feeling like you never truly get a break. Long hours at the office and constantly being tied to your phones and emails at home prevent work-life balance. Trying to create time for yourself while balancing the demands of work with your own needs and responsibilities outside the office is also a constant source of stress.

Another important stressor is the uncertainty in the economic climate, the fear of layoffs, restructuring, or job loss, which is job insecurity. It fuels anxiety and stress by weighing heavily on your mind. You will agree with me that it is hard to stay motivated when you are constantly worried about whether you will still have a job tomorrow. Imagine you are at work and you are worried about the economic recession. You check your LinkedIn, and you hear stories of layoffs from major companies, so you are constantly lying on a bed of nails, wondering when the layoff will get to your company.

Last but certainly not least, have you ever wondered why you feel exhausted, disillusioned, and utterly drained every day? You are experiencing the ever-present burnout! This happens when you push yourself to the limit day in and day out without sufficient rest or time to recharge. This is particularly common when you work in a fast-paced company, get paid hourly, or even run multiple jobs. You are in a race against time, so you have no time left for yourself, and this affects you both mentally and physically.

Parenting: Challenges and Sources of Parental Stress

Parenting, oh parenting! It is one of those things everyone seems to have an opinion on, right? When you talk about parenting stress, there are people in your social circle who think, "Why have kids when you cannot deal with the stress?" or "It is normal. Stress comes with having kids." Unfortunately, none of these schools of thought really solve your problem.

If you are a parent, you are probably nodding your head vigorously right now. The struggle is real, my friend! From sleepless nights with a crying baby to the constant juggling act of work, household chores, and keeping your little ones from turning your living room into a war zone, it is no wonder parents often feel like they are on the verge of losing their minds.

However, where does all this stress come from? For starters, there is the pressure to be the perfect parent. You know, the one who bakes homemade organic snacks, volunteers at every school event, and never raises their voice in frustration. Yeah, good luck with that!

Then there is the whole "balancing act" thing. Trying to find that sweet spot between spending quality time with your kids and not completely neglecting your own needs is like walking blindfolded. Also, let us not even get started on the constant worry about whether you are doing enough to set your kids up for success in life. That is enough to keep any parent awake at night.

There is also the never-ending stream of unsolicited advice from well-meaning friends, family members, and random strangers on the internet. Apparently, everyone and their dog have a foolproof method for getting your kid to eat their broccoli or stop throwing tantrums in the middle of the grocery store. They also have more than enough time on their hands to tell you how to parent your own kids while you have to smile through their entire advice.

I know it is crazy, but hey, you are not alone; every parent out there is facing their own set of challenges and dealing with their own sources of stress. Cut yourself some slack, and, of course, keep reading because we are in this together.

Strategies for Managing Work and Parenting Stressors

Parenting and professional life often come with endless demands and deadlines competing for your attention. In the midst of this, it is easy to neglect your own well-being. Below are some strategies to manage work and parenting stress; enjoy!

Self-care

Did self-care just make you think of luxurious spa days or bubble baths? Well, it is much more than pampering yourself or indulging in leisure activities, although those are important too. As a professional, it is about how you intentionally prioritize and nurture your mental, emotional, and physical well-being. It helps you recognize when you need to hit pause and give yourself the tender love and care you deserve while you are juggling deadlines, meetings, and a never-ending to-do list.

As a parent, it's about how you acknowledge your own needs and make them a priority alongside your children's. Carving out time amidst school runs, soccer practices, and household chores is not just beneficial for you; it is essential for your entire family. When you take care of yourself, you are better equipped to handle the challenges of parenting with patience and grace.

As both a parent and a professional, find moments in your day to replenish your energy reserves and recharge your spirit. Whether it is a brief meditation session in the morning, a walk during your lunch break, or simply setting boundaries to protect your downtime, every small act of self-care adds up.

So, don't spend the whole day fastening baby bibs and getting files to your superior. Be intentional about prioritizing your self-care and discover what works best for you. Shift your perspective on self-care from being just another item on your to-do list to an integral part of your daily routine, and when you prioritize, do not dare cancel out self-care. You will be tempted, but don't cancel it. By nurturing yourself, you are not only enhancing your own resilience but also setting a powerful example for your children and fostering a healthier, happier family dynamic.

Time Management

Many of us think we are managing well by stuffing more tasks into our day or creating elaborate schedules that we cannot stick to. My dear, that is not it. Time management is about finding the balance between productivity and well-being while tackling both your work and parenting duties without constantly lagging behind. It is about prioritizing your tasks, understanding your peak productivity hours, and learning when to say no. It makes sure that you have time for work, time for yourself, and even time for the kids. I know it sounds too good to be true, but it is possible.

How do you do this? First, write down everything that needs to be done, both at work and at home. Prioritize the tasks and allocate time for them to avoid forgetting something important. Next, set clear boundaries between work time and family time. Very clear boundaries mean no work emails or work discussions at the dinner table... not even if your husband is your boss. When you are at work, focus on work, and when you are with your family, be present in the moment. Give each aspect of your life the attention it deserves without letting one bleed into the other. Give this a try and watch as your stress melts away bit by bit.

Time Off and Vacation

You have probably planned on taking time off a million times, but somehow, you get lost in the shuffle of everyday life. This is your cue to get the time off and vacation you deserve!

When I say "time off," I don't just mean clocking out at the end of the day or just sipping margaritas by the pool (although that does sound pretty enticing). I am talking about intentional, guilt-free, leave-your-worries-at-the-door kind of time off. Whether it is a mental health day to recharge your batteries or a long weekend getaway with the family, carving out space for yourself is important for both your physical and mental well-being.

Alternatively, you can plan a vacation to escape the emails, meetings, and the endless chorus of "Mom, Dad, I need..." for a blissful moment of peace and relaxation. Whether you are lounging on a beach, exploring a new city, or simply enjoying a stay in your own backyard, just make sure you get the much-needed break from the daily routine.

Effective Communication

Communication is about actively listening, expressing your thoughts and feelings, and understanding those of others. It holds teams and families together and ensures everyone is on the same page.

At work, whenever you are feeling overwhelmed and buried with tasks, there is a likelihood your colleagues are, too. So, we need to lighten up the mood. Don't be that uptight guy who is always talking about deadlines and making everyone uncomfortable. Instead, be the guy that opens up the line of communication. When you open up lines of communication, you create an opportunity for everyone to voice their concerns, share their workload, and offer support. Suddenly, those pending deadlines won't seem so insurmountable when you have a team rallying behind you. Be proactive in seeking feedback, clarifying expectations, and addressing conflicts head-on. Misunderstandings, conflicts, and feeling isolated are common stressors in the workplace, and communication serves as a powerful antidote to these challenges.

At the home front, communicating openly and honestly with your partner and kids or even seeking support from other parents can make all the difference. Communication is not just about talking; it is also about walking the walk. Reach out, share your thoughts, and ask for support. When you are transparent about your needs and boundaries, you will have a better relationship with others.

Personal Development

When you are faced with tight deadlines at work or tantrums at home, having a strong foundation of personal development can help you stay grounded and focused. Not everyone was born a good communicator or time manager. Sometimes, we have to acquire these skills. While personal development skills like prioritizing tasks and setting boundaries work wonders in reducing workplace stress, effective communication and patience come in handy in parenting. However, personal development goes beyond acquiring skills; it encompasses your mind's mental and emotional well-being. Personal development is a journey, not a destination, so experiment with different strategies to find what works best for you. Whether it is attending workshops, reading self-help books, or seeking guidance from a mentor, there are endless opportunities for growth. Embrace the journey, invest in yourself, and watch as you emerge stronger than ever before. You've got this!

In this chapter, we have discussed the common stressors in adult life and shed more light on the intricacies of managing both professional responsibilities and the challenges of parenting. From workplace stressors like tight deadlines, work overload, and difficult relationships to the constant demands of parenting, each aspect contributes to the complexity of our adult life. We have shed light on common workplace stressors and have highlighted the importance of recognizing and addressing these challenges proactively. We also looked at how to address them. In the next chapter, we will be looking at how to identify signs and symptoms of stress.

Chapter 4

Identifying Signs of Stress and Anxiety

Can you truly pinpoint the signs of stress and anxiety when they arise within you? While many of us think we know what these feelings entail, there is often so much we do not know. Recognizing the signs of stress and anxiety is not always as straightforward as we might assume. Sure, we have all heard about racing thoughts, sleepless nights, or feeling on edge, but there is a spectrum to these experiences. Sometimes, the signs can be subtle. In this chapter, we will be discussing how to identify signs of stress and anxiety.

Common Symptoms of Stress and Anxiety

You might be thinking, "I know stress and anxiety; I've felt them before." But do you really know all the ways they can show up in your life? Let us look at some common symptoms so you can spot them even when they are hiding in plain sight.

1. Physical Signs:

The tightness in your chest, rapid heartbeat, and tense muscles are not meant to be overlooked. These are classic signs of stress and anxiety. Sometimes, you might feel like there's a weight pressing down on your chest, making it hard to breathe, or you are sitting in a conference room and your heart is beating so fast it feels like you ran 16 km per hour on a treadmill. This rapid heartbeat is a common physical response to stress and anxiety, and it is triggered by your body's fight-or-flight response. Dr. Smith, a renowned psychiatrist, notes that our bodies often react to stress before our minds even realize it. So, pay attention to those aches, pains, and subtle signs.

2. Sleep Troubles:

You crawl into bed exhausted, but as soon as your head hits the pillow, your mind starts racing. Hours pass by, and you find yourself tossing and turning, unable to find a comfortable position or quiet your thoughts. So, as a hardworking Jack or Jill, you get out of bed and do some of the work left over from the office. Stop it!

You see, sleep disturbances are closely linked to stress and anxiety. Dr. Annise Wilson, a sleep expert at Baylor College of Medicine, says stress can affect sleep in many ways, and the most common one we see is insomnia. So, if you find yourself counting sheep more often than catching sleep, stress might be the culprit. Of course, you know the solution to stress is not doing more work, so if you find yourself in this position, do not pick up work left from the office.

3. Changes in Appetite:

Your favorite meal is sitting in front of you, but the thought of eating makes your stomach churn, or you find yourself reaching for sugary snacks or salty treats more often than usual. It can be because of stress.

Stress triggers cravings for comfort foods, which provide a temporary escape from overwhelming emotions. However, it can also be an appetite stealer. According to the American Psychological Association, stress can alter overall food intake in two ways, resulting in under- or overeating, which may be influenced by stressor severity. The organization also points out that chronic life stress seems to be associated with a greater preference for energy- and nutrient-dense foods, namely those that are high in sugar and fat. So, if your relationship with food feels wrong, it could be a red flag for stress or anxiety.

4. Mood Swings:

You are having a great time with friends, laughing and joking around, but then you suddenly feel sad for no apparent reason. You may also notice that small inconveniences that you would normally brush off now send you into a fit of anger. Stress can wear down your patience, leaving you feeling irritable and easily agitated. Dr. Cara Gardenswartz, a clinical psychologist and founder of Group Therapy LA and Group Therapy NY, said that stressful life events or stages of life can make people more prone to mood swings. So, if you are feeling like you are on an emotional rollercoaster, it might be a sign of stress.

5. Difficulty Concentrating:

Sometimes, you walk into a room with a purpose in mind, but as soon as you enter the room, you forget why you are there. You can also find it hard to focus during meetings, classes, while playing games, or even when driving. According to the World

Health Organization (WHO), stress makes it difficult to concentrate. So, if you are finding it harder to stay on task, it might be an indicator of stress.

Although the above are some common indicators of stress and anxiety, you cannot just write off every single one of the things above as stress-induced. For example, forgetfulness and lack of concentration can be due to different factors.

Self-assessment Exercises

Identify Personal Stressors

Stressors vary from person to person, and the degree of disturbance of each stressor is also different. What gets under my skin might not bother you at all, and vice versa. This is why it is necessary to know your own personal stressors. However, finding out your own stressors can be hard. So, here's the deal: I have compiled some self-assessment exercises for you. These exercises were compiled based on different paid and free tools for identifying stressors. I carried out the research, so you don't have to!

Self-Assessment Exercise 1: Reflecting on Daily Triggers

If you want to reduce your load of stress, you might want to start by identifying the specific things that cause this stress. Take a moment to reflect on your daily life and identify the specific triggers that contribute to your stress levels. Below is a list of questions that can set you on the right track. Make sure each of your answers is written or typed because you still have to revisit them. Of course, remember to be honest with yourself.

1. What specific tasks or responsibilities tend to evoke stress or anxiety for me throughout the day?

2. Are there particular people or interactions that consistently leave me feeling drained or frustrated?

3. How do I typically respond to unexpected challenges or changes in my routine?

4. Do certain environments or settings trigger feelings of discomfort or tension?

5. Are there recurring thoughts or worries that preoccupy my mind during the day?

6. How do I feel during peak stress periods, and how does it impact my ability to focus or perform tasks?

7. Are there any patterns or themes among the situations that consistently lead to an overwhelming feeling?

8. How do I typically cope with stressors in the moment, and do these strategies effectively alleviate or exacerbate my feelings of stress?

9. Are there moments of the day when I feel particularly calm or content, and what factors contribute to these positive experiences?

10. Reflecting on my daily triggers, what adjustments or changes could I make to minimize stress and enhance my overall well-being?

After answering these questions, carefully look at what you have written. See if there is any common pattern among the triggers you have identified. If there is any, then you might want to look at that. For example, if your answer to number 4 is your workplace, your answer to number 5 is work deadlines, and your answer to number 2 is your superior, then you might want to consider your job as a possible source of stress.

Self-Assessment Exercise 2: Exploring Emotional Responses

Earlier in this book, we already established the fact that stress can influence our emotions. This is exactly why this exercise was added because by looking at how our emotions fluctuate, we may get an insight into the nature of the stressors causing our emotions to fluctuate. As with the first exercise, make sure answers to these questions are written or typed.

1. What emotions have I been experiencing most frequently?

2. Are there specific situations or triggers that consistently elicit strong emotional responses?

3. How do I typically react when I encounter stressful or challenging situations?

4. Do I tend to suppress or ignore my emotions, or do I allow myself to fully experience and express them?

5. Are there certain emotions that I find difficult to acknowledge or accept? If so, why?

6. Have I noticed any patterns in my emotional responses during different times of the day or week?

7. How do my emotions impact my interactions with others and my overall well-being?

8. Do I have healthy coping mechanisms in place for dealing with intense emotions, or do I tend to resort to unhealthy behaviors?

9. Are there any recurring themes or underlying issues that seem to be contributing to my emotional distress?

10. What strategies can I implement to better regulate my emotions and cultivate greater emotional resilience?

After answering these questions, once again, check your responses to see if there is any trend. If there is any situation that causes you to have negative emotions, you might want to look into that.

Self-Assessment Exercise 3: Analyzing Physical Symptoms

Finally, we are asking questions where we listen to our body now because, of course, your body knows best! So let us listen to our body by asking these questions:

1. Headaches and Migraines:

- Have you experienced any headaches or migraines recently? If so, how often do they occur, and are there any patterns or triggers you've noticed?

- Are these headaches accompanied by other symptoms such as nausea, sensitivity to light or sound, or visual disturbances?

2. Muscle Tension:

- Do you frequently notice tension or tightness in specific areas of your body, such as your neck, shoulders, or back?

- Are there particular activities or situations that tend to exacerbate muscle tension, such as sitting at a desk for long periods or engaging in strenuous physical activity?

3. Sleep Disturbances:

- How would you rate the quality of your sleep on a scale of 1 to 10, with 1 being poor and 10 being excellent?

- Do you have difficulty falling asleep, staying asleep, or waking up feeling refreshed?

- Are there any specific stressors or worries that tend to disrupt your sleep patterns?

4. Gastrointestinal Issues:

- Have you experienced any digestive problems such as stomachaches, bloating, or changes in bowel habits?

- Do these symptoms coincide with periods of heightened stress or anxiety?

5. Changes in Appetite:

- Have you noticed any changes in your appetite or eating habits recently, such as overeating, undereating, or cravings for specific foods?

- Do these changes correspond to periods of increased stress or emotional distress?

6. Fatigue and Low Energy:

- Do you often feel fatigued or lacking in energy, even after a full night's sleep?

- Are there specific times of day

Answering 'Yes' to more than half of the questions in each segment is a possible indication of stress. However, this is not definitive. This is because physical symptoms are often caused by a combination of various factors. Also, in places where you listed certain triggers or situations, look at those situations and see if there is a trend.

In this chapter, we looked at some common symptoms of stress as well as some self-assessment exercises. In the next chapter, we will be looking at practical techniques to deal with stress.

Chapter 5

Practical Techniques to Deal with Stress

Since the beginning of this book, we have been talking about stress and stressors. However, we have not really discussed how to deal with them. This chapter will cover that. Before we delve in, it is good to remember that stressors cannot be completely eradicated, but we can cope with them. We also need to know that sometimes, stress can spiral out of control and affect our physical and mental health. It is, therefore, necessary that we know how to deal with it. Below are some practical techniques for dealing with stress.

Deep Breathing Exercises

We breathe all the time, don't we? So, what's the hassle with deep breathing? Well, deep breathing is an intentional action, and you cannot compare it to your regular breathing, which is subconscious. The difference between the two is like the difference between scribbling and actually writing. Deep breathing is not just about inhaling and exhaling; it is about tapping into the power of your breath to calm your mind and body.

How does it work? In 1975, Herbert Benson coined the term "The Relaxation Response", which describes how short periods of meditation that focus on breathing can alter the body's stress response. When you take slow, deep breaths, you are sending a signal to your brain that it is time to chill out. It is like hitting the reset button on your stress levels. With each breath, you are flooding your body with oxygen, which helps relax your muscles and slow down your heart rate. Sounds cool, right? So let us go ahead and break down how to do deep breathing for stress reduction:

Step 1: Find a quiet place

Start by finding a quiet and comfortable space where you can sit or lie down without any distractions.

Step 2: Get Comfortable

Sit in a comfortable position with your back straight, or lie down on your back with your arms resting at your sides.

Step 3: Relax Your Muscles

Take a moment to relax your muscles, starting from your toes and working your way up to your shoulders and neck. Let go of any tension you may be holding onto.

Step 4: Focus on Your Breath

Close your eyes if it helps you to relax and bring your attention to your breath. Take a few normal breaths to settle in.

Step 5: Inhale Slowly Through Your Nose

Begin by inhaling slowly and deeply through your nose. Feel your abdomen rise as you fill your lungs with air. Aim to breathe in for a count of about four seconds.

Step 6: Hold Your Breath

Once you've inhaled fully, pause for a moment and hold your breath for a count of two seconds. This allows the oxygen to circulate throughout your body.

Step 7: Exhale Slowly Through Your Mouth

Now, exhale slowly and completely through your mouth. Feel your abdomen deflate as you release the air from your lungs. Aim to exhale for a count of about six seconds.

Step 8: Repeat

Continue this pattern of deep breathing for several minutes, focusing on the rhythm of your breath and the sensation of relaxation with each exhale.

Step 9: Stay Present

As you practice deep breathing, try to stay present in the moment and let go of any distracting thoughts. If your mind wanders, gently bring your focus back to your breath.

Step 10: Practice Regularly

Deep breathing should be a regular part of your routine, especially during times of stress or when you need to calm your mind. The more you practice, the more effective it will become in reducing stress and promoting relaxation.

Deep breathing is a simple and powerful tool for stress

reduction. Take a few moments each day to practice and reap the benefits of a calmer and more centered mind.

Nutrition As a Way of Stress Relief

You have likely heard the importance of nutrition for your physical health countless times. However, do you know that what you eat can also significantly impact your stress levels and overall mental well-being? It is true! If you don't trust me, then I'm going to quote someone you will most likely trust.

Dr. Elissa Epel, Professor and Vice Chair of the Department of Psychiatry and Behavioral Sciences at the University of California, San Francisco, said that just as stress can affect nutrition, nutrition can also affect stress. To prove this, Dr. Epel discussed the results of population-based studies that found that dietary patterns emphasizing whole foods were associated with lower depression, anxiety, and stress, whereas a typical Western dietary pattern was associated with a higher risk of poor mental health.

Are you surprised? I know when we talk about stress relief, our minds often jump to meditation, exercise, or maybe even a relaxing bubble bath, but what about the food on our plates? It turns out that what we eat plays a crucial role in how our bodies handle stress. Think about it this way: your body is like a machine, and food is the fuel that keeps it running smoothly. In the same way, putting low-quality fuel in a car can cause it to sputter and stall; filling your body with junk food can lead to

45

increased stress levels and a foggy mind.

So, what should you be eating to keep stress at bay? You can incorporate plenty of fruits, vegetables, whole grains, and lean proteins into your diet. This can provide your body with the nutrients it needs to stay resilient in the face of stress. However, it is not just about what you eat; it is also about how you eat. Taking the time to sit down and enjoy a meal can help to reduce stress levels and improve digestion. So, put away the screens, take a deep breath, and savor each bite. Also, it is not about food alone. Dehydration can exacerbate feelings of stress and fatigue, so be sure to drink plenty of water throughout the day to keep your body and mind in top shape.

While nutrition may not be the first thing that comes to mind when you think about stress relief, it is certainly worth paying attention to. So, the next time you are feeling stressed out, consider reaching for a nutritious snack instead of that bag of chips. Your body and mind will thank you for it!

Exercise for Stress Relief

Apart from nutrition, exercise is another way of relieving stress. Now, you're probably thinking, "Isn't exercise stressful?" Well, stick around while some of your possible questions get answered.

What's the deal with exercise and stress relief?

When you work up a sweat, your body releases endorphins. Those feel-good chemicals can then lift your mood.

How does it work?

It is all about giving your body and mind a break from whatever is stressing you out. When you are focusing on your workout, you are not dwelling on your worries. Also, exercise can help lower your levels of cortisol, the stress hormone, leaving you feeling more relaxed.

What kind of exercise should you do?

The great thing is there is no one-size-fits-all answer. Whether you are into yoga, running, dancing, or hitting the gym, the important thing is to find something you enjoy. That way, you will be more likely to stick with it and reap the stress-busting benefits.

How much exercise do you need?

Aim for at least 30 minutes of moderate-intensity exercise most days of the week. But hey, if you can't fit in a full workout, even a quick walk around the block can help take the edge off.

Are there any other perks apart from stress reduction?

Absolutely! Regular exercise can also improve your sleep, boost your confidence, and give you more energy to tackle whatever life throws your way. So, really, what's not to love?

There you have it – how you can use exercise to kick the stress out. Give it a try and see how much better you feel!

Mindfulness Meditation

Mindfulness meditation involves bringing one's attention to the present moment intentionally and without judgment. It emphasizes awareness of thoughts, feelings, bodily sensations, and the surrounding environment. Through regular practice, you can cultivate a state of mindfulness, which can lead to increased clarity, calmness, and resilience.

Many studies have investigated the effects of mindfulness meditation on stress reduction and mental health. The findings of these studies suggest that regular practice of mindfulness meditation can lead to significant improvements in stress levels, anxiety, depression, and overall psychological functioning. Neuroscientific studies have also revealed changes in brain structure and function associated with mindfulness meditation, including increased activity in regions responsible for attention, emotion regulation, and self-awareness.

So, how can mindfulness meditation be incorporated into daily life as a means of dealing with stress? One approach is to establish a regular meditation practice, dedicating a few minutes each day to mindfulness exercises. This can involve focusing on the breath, body scan meditations, or simply observing thoughts and emotions without attachment. You can also incorporate mindfulness into everyday activities, like eating, walking, or engaging in conversations, as a way to enhance present-moment awareness and reduce stress levels.

Now that we understand a bit about mindfulness meditation let us explore how to integrate this practice into our daily lives:

1. **Start Small:** Begin with just a few minutes of mindfulness meditation each day and gradually increase the duration as you become more comfortable with the practice.

2. **Find a Quiet Space:** Choose a quiet and comfortable environment where you can sit or lie down without distractions.

3. **Focus on the Breath:** Pay attention to the sensations of your breath as it moves in and out of your body. You can focus on the rise and fall of your chest or the feeling of air passing through your nostrils. Be conscious and pay attention. It is called mindfulness meditation for a reason.

4. **Notice Your Thoughts:** When thoughts arise during meditation, simply observe them without judgment and gently redirect your focus back to your breath.

5. **Practice Regularly:** Consistency is key to reaping the benefits of mindfulness meditation. Set aside time each day for your practice, even if it's just a few minutes.

Practicing Gratitude

Practicing gratitude goes beyond merely saying "thank you" for something received. It involves a deeper appreciation for the positive aspects of our lives, big and small. It also involves recognizing the sources of goodness in our world. Summarily, it is about cultivating a mindset of appreciation and focusing on what we have rather than what we lack. So, instead of thinking about how you cannot get the Chanel bag you want, think about the beautiful Fenty lipstick you got for Christmas.

Now, let us look at how practicing gratitude can help us better cope with stress. You see, research suggests that gratitude has a multitude of benefits for our mental and emotional well-being. By shifting our focus from what is going wrong to what is going right, gratitude reframes our perspective and enhances our ability to face challenges. It acts as a counterbalance to negativity bias and reduces the tendency to dwell on the negative aspects of our lives while overlooking the positive.

So, how can we incorporate gratitude into our daily lives? The good news is that gratitude is a skill that can be cultivated through simple practices. Here are some practical strategies to get started:

1. **Gratitude Journaling**: Set aside a few minutes each day to write down three things you are grateful for. They can be as small as a warm cup of coffee in the morning or as significant as a supportive friend.

2. **Gratitude Reflection**: Take a moment before bed to reflect on the day and identify moments of gratitude. Recalling positive experiences can help shift your focus away from stressors and promote a sense of peace.

3. **Expressing Thanks**: Do not hesitate to express gratitude to those around you. A heartfelt "thank you" can strengthen relationships and form a sense of connection.

4. **Mindful Appreciation**: Incorporate mindfulness into your gratitude practice by paying attention to the present moment and savoring the simple pleasures of life. Whether it is a beautiful sunset or a delicious meal, fully immerse yourself in the experience.

In this chapter, we were able to look at some practical techniques for dealing with stress. We looked at exercise, nutrition, mindfulness, and practicing gratitude. In the next chapter, we will be moving to the mental wellness session, so don't get tired yet; it is about to get more interesting.

MENTAL WELLNESS

Chapter 6

The Mind-Body Connection: How Mental Health Impacts Physical Well-being

In Chapter 2, it was established that our mental health influences our physical well-being. However, we did not discuss how. In this chapter, we will be doing just that.

What is the Mind-Body Connection?

On the surface, it sounds pretty straightforward: the mind and body are connected, right? But there's more to it than meets the eye. Think about it for a moment. When you are stressed out, do you notice how your body reacts? Maybe your heart races, your muscles tense up, or you get a headache. That is the mind-body connection in action. Your thoughts and emotions can have a real, tangible impact on your physical health.

However, it goes both ways. Just as your mind can influence your body, your body can also influence your mind. Ever noticed how a good workout can lift your mood? That is because physical activity releases endorphins– those feel-good chemicals in your brain. So, the mind-body connection is not just some abstract concept—it is a fundamental aspect of our health and well-being.

What Experts Have to Say:

The mind-body connection is not an assumption or some people's idea. It is an actual scientific concept that has been proven by a number of experts. So, let's see what some experts have to say about it.

Dr. Herbert Benson

> *"The mind and body are not separate units but one integrated system. How we think and feel influences how we behave and, ultimately, our health outcomes."*

Dr. Benson, a pioneer in mind-body medicine and the founder of the Benson-Henry Institute for Mind-Body Medicine, emphasizes the impact of relaxation techniques on both mental and physical health. He famously coined the term "the relaxation response" to describe the body's natural counterpart to the stress response. According to Dr. Benson, practices such as meditation and deep breathing can induce a state of deep relaxation, leading to physiological changes that promote overall well-being.

Dr. Candace Pert

> *"Your body is your subconscious mind. Our physical body can be changed by the emotions we experience."*

As a neuroscientist and pharmacologist, Dr. Pert's research focused on the connections between emotions, the brain, and the immune system. She discovered the presence of neuropeptides, or "molecules of emotion," throughout the body, linking emotional states to physiological responses. Dr. Pert's work highlights the bidirectional communication between the mind and body, suggesting that emotions can influence health outcomes.

Dr. Jon Kabat-Zinn

"Mindfulness means paying attention in a particular way: on purpose, in the present moment, and non-judgmentally. This kind of attention nurtures greater awareness, clarity, and acceptance of present-moment reality."

Known for his work in mindfulness-based stress reduction (MBSR), Dr. Kabat-Zinn emphasizes the importance of mindfulness practices in fostering mind-body awareness and resilience. He believes that cultivating present-moment awareness can lead to a deeper understanding of the mind-body connection and promote holistic well-being.

The works of these people and many others contributed to understanding the relationship between the mind and the body. However, the mind-body relationship is not without its own criticism. For example, some scientists and researchers remain skeptical of the mind-body connection due to the complexities of studying subjective experiences like emotions and consciousness. So, they argue that the evidence supporting the mind-body connection is insufficient or inconclusive. Certain individuals also adhere to a reductionist perspective, which seeks to explain complex phenomena solely in terms of their constituent parts. From this viewpoint, the mind-body connection may be dismissed as an oversimplification or pseudoscience because it involves integrating psychological and physiological factors that are traditionally studied in separate disciplines.

Nonetheless, even with these criticisms, the mind-body connection is still a widely accepted scientific concept.

The Bidirectional Relationship Between Mental Health and Physical Health

Mental health refers to our emotional, psychological, and social well-being, while physical health relates to our body's overall condition and functioning. Seems pretty straightforward, but here's the kicker – these two are not just chilling in their own separate lanes. They are actually intertwined in ways that might surprise you.

First up, let us talk about how our mental state can affect our physical well-being. Stress, anxiety, and depression can wreak havoc on your body. When you are stressed out or feeling down, your body releases all sorts of fun chemicals like cortisol and adrenaline, which can mess with your immune system and increase inflammation. And guess what? Chronic inflammation has been linked to a whole host of health problems, including heart disease, diabetes, and even cancer!

Unfortunately, there is more. Studies have shown that people with mental health disorders are also more likely to engage in unhealthy behaviors like smoking, drinking, and overeating. These habits can take a serious toll on their physical health. Over time, they can lead to things like obesity, high blood pressure, and respiratory issues. So yes, your mental health can definitely impact your physical health in some pretty big ways.

Now, let us flip the script and talk about how your physical health can affect your mental well-being. Believe it or not, taking care of your body is not just good for your waistline; it is also crucial for your mental health. For example, as mentioned in Chapter 5, regular exercise has been shown to release endorphins, aka the "feel-good" hormones, which can boost your mood and reduce feelings of anxiety and depression. Also, getting those endorphins flowing can help you sleep better, which is key for maintaining good mental health.

However, that is not all. Research has also found that certain nutrients, like omega-3 fatty acids found in fish and vitamins like B12 and D, play a role in brain health and can help prevent or alleviate symptoms of mental health disorders. So, yes, what you eat can definitely affect how you feel.

Now, you might be wondering, "What's going on in my body to make this all happen?" Well, scientists have been busy studying the brain-body connection, and they have uncovered some pretty fascinating stuff. Turns out, there is this thing called the hypothalamic-pituitary-adrenal (HPA) axis, which controls our body's response to stress. When we are under pressure, the HPA axis goes into overdrive, releasing stress hormones that can impact everything, from our immune system to our digestion.

However, this is where it gets really interesting. The HPA axis does not just respond to external stressors; it is also influenced by our thoughts, emotions, and behaviors. So, when we are feeling anxious or depressed, it can set off a chain reaction in our bodies that affects our physical health.

There you have it – the bidirectional relationship between mental and physical health in all its glory! It is clear that these physical and mental health are not just distant cousins. They are more like inseparable best friends who influence each other in many ways. Whether you are sweating it out at the gym or practicing mindfulness meditation, taking care of your mind and body is crucial for overall well-being. So, next time you are feeling a little off, remember that it is not just in your head; it is in your body, too.

In this chapter, we explored the connection between the mind and the body and physical and mental health. In the next chapter, we will be looking at healthy practices for mental wellness.

Chapter 7

Healthy Practices for Mental Wellness

Healthy practice is important for maintaining a healthy mind and embracing mental wellness. In this chapter, we will be exploring two fundamental pillars of mental health: Self-care Practices and Sleep Hygiene. I am going to let you in on some super cool ideas and practices that can help you nurture your mental health and turn little habits and routines into a big difference in how you feel every day. Let's get started!

Self-care Practices for Mental Wellness

Just like you would not expect your car to keep running smoothly without regular maintenance, you should not expect yourself to function at your best without taking care of your needs. That is where self-care comes in. Self-care is an ongoing practice of committing, prioritizing your well-being day in and day out, and being kind to yourself even on the toughest days. You can go for a walk in nature to clear your head, practice mindfulness or meditation to center yourself, or simply indulge in your favorite hobbies to recharge your batteries. Engaging in these activities will bring you joy and fulfillment, help you reduce stress, boost your mood, and increase your overall sense of wellness.

Self-Care Activities for Physical, Emotional, and Spiritual Well-Being

Self-care includes several strategies to help you navigate the ups and downs of life. Below are some self-care activities for your physical, emotional, and spiritual well-being.

Self-Care Activities for Your Physical Well-Being

Physical well-being includes everything that keeps your body feeling good and functioning at its best. You have probably heard about exercise and eating right a million times; that is the basics of physical wellbeing. So I am sorry, but I have to mention them again.

As said earlier, exercise is an important aspect of physical well-being. Fortunately, it does not have to mean slogging away on a treadmill for hours. It can be as simple as taking a walk, dancing around your living room, or trying out a new workout video on YouTube.

Now, how exactly do you exercise without nourishing your body with good food? There is no way! Swap out processed snacks for fresh fruits and veggies, or cook a homemade meal instead of ordering takeout.

Apart from eating good food and exercising, there is sleep. Cheating nature will take its toll on you one day. So, put down your phone, stop the Netflix marathon, and give your body the rest it deserves. Ultimately, pamper yourself! Find what feels

60

good for you and make it a regular part of your routine.

Self-Care Activities for Your Emotional Well-Being

It is essential to take care of your mental health just as much as your physical health. One way to do this is by practicing *mindfulness and self-compassion.* Take a few moments each day to check in with yourself. How are you feeling? What do you need right now? And remember, it is okay not to be okay sometimes. Give yourself permission to feel your emotions fully without judgment.

Another way is *journaling;* pouring out your thoughts and feelings on pages is therapeutic. You can write about your day, your dreams, your fears – whatever is on your mind. Additionally, *connecting with loved ones* is incredibly nourishing for your emotional well-being. Reach out to a friend or family member and have a heart-to-heart chat. Sometimes, just talking things out with someone who cares about you can make a world of difference.

Self-Care Activities for Your Spiritual Well-Being

Lastly, let us talk about spiritual well-being. Before we continue, it is great to note that this does not necessarily mean religion (although it can if that's your thing). Spiritual well-being is about connecting with something greater than yourself—whether that is nature, art, music, or your own inner wisdom.

Now, let's move on to self-care activities to nurture your spiritual well-being. One great way to start is by setting aside some quiet time each day for *reflection*. This could be through meditation, prayer, journaling, or simply sitting in silence and allowing your mind to wander. Another powerful self-care activity is *spending time in nature*. Whether it is going for a hike in the mountains, taking a stroll through the park, or simply sitting in your backyard and listening to the bird's chirp, being in nature can help you feel more connected to the world around you and tap into a deeper sense of spirituality.

Engaging in *acts of kindness and compassion* is another fantastic way to nurture your spiritual well-being. This could be anything from volunteering at a local charity, helping out a friend in need, or simply smiling at a stranger on the street. By practicing kindness and empathy towards others, you not only make the world a better place but also cultivate a sense of inner peace and fulfillment within yourself.

In addition, *self-expression* through art, music, dance, or any other creative outlet, of expressing yourself can be incredibly nourishing for your spiritual well-being. So don't be afraid to let your creative juices flow and explore new forms of self-expression.

Lastly, *the power of connection* surrounding yourself with supportive friends and family members who uplift and inspire you can be a powerful form of self-care. So, make time for meaningful conversations and moments of laughter and joy with the people you love.

Overall, just take time to engage in activities that feed your soul. Find what brings you a sense of peace and purpose, and make it a regular part of your self-care routine.

Creating A Personalized Self-Care Plan

I know we have been throwing around the word "Self-care" all around in this book, but so far, there has been nothing regarding how to plan it. We will be remedying that now. Here, I will be taking you through step by step on creating a self-care plan tailored to suit your needs.

Step 1: Reflect on Your Needs

Think about it. When was the last time you really sat down and thought about what you need to take care of yourself? I am talking about deep, introspective reflection on your physical, emotional, and mental needs. It's been a long time, right? Well, in that case, grab a cozy spot or a cup of tea, and let's get real.

What do you need right now to feel balanced, fulfilled, and happy? It's okay if it takes you a while to figure it out. I know you probably haven't thought about it before. That's fine. We are all guilty of putting our needs on the back burner sometimes. Do you need more sleep? More time for hobbies? Maybe you're craving more meaningful connections with loved ones. Or perhaps you're feeling overwhelmed and need to set some boundaries to protect your mental health. Whatever it is, take the time to acknowledge it and jot them down.

Step 2: Identify Your Triggers for Your Self-Care Plan

Alright, so you have decided to dive into the world of self-care. Great choice! However, to make a holistic plan, you need to know your triggers. Triggers are the things that set off your stress alarm, sending you spiraling into a state of overwhelm or anxiety. Unless you know what those triggers are, there is no moving forward. It could be certain tasks, environments, or even people. Recognizing your triggers is the first step to managing them effectively. So, grab a pen and paper (or your phone, if you're more tech-savvy) and let us get to work. Start by reflecting on your day. What moments make you feel tense or frazzled? Is it that never-ending pile of emails? The commute? Or certain people or situations that just rub you the wrong way. Write it all down with no judgment, and take a deep breath. You have just taken a huge step towards building a self-care plan that actually works for you.

Step 3: Set Realistic Goals

Now that you know what you need and what stresses you out, it is time to set some goals. Let's get this! Setting goals is like laying the foundation for a strong house. You want something solid to build upon, something that will not crumble under pressure. So, what exactly are realistic goals when it comes to self-care?

First, think about what you can actually achieve. It is easy to get caught up in the excitement of making big changes, but if those changes are too drastic or overwhelming, you are setting yourself up for disappointment. Instead, aim for small, manageable steps that you can realistically incorporate into your daily routine. For example, maybe you want to start meditating every day to help reduce stress. Instead of saying you will meditate for an hour each morning (let us be real, who has the time?), start with just five minutes a day. It might not seem like much, but trust me, even a few minutes of mindfulness can work wonders.

Another thing to consider is your current circumstances. Life can be unpredictable, and sometimes, things just do not go as planned. That is why it is important to be flexible with your goals. If you find yourself getting overwhelmed or falling behind, do not be afraid to adjust your expectations. Self-care is not about perfection; it is about doing the best you can with what you have.

Step 4: Make a Plan

Once you've set your goals, it is time to create a plan of action. Grab a pen and paper or your favorite note-taking app because it is time to make a plan that is all about YOU. First, identify the activities that make you feel recharged, energized, and ready to take on the world. Once you have the list of activities that resonate with you, it is time to make a plan. Think about how you can incorporate these activities into your daily or weekly routine and treat them like appointments that you cannot miss. Maybe you schedule a morning yoga session before work or set aside time on the weekends for a hobby you love. Sometimes, sticking to a self-care routine is easier said than done. If you miss a day or two, that is okay! Just pick yourself back up and keep going. Also, check in with yourself regularly. How are you feeling? Are you prioritizing your self-care? If not, what can you do to get back on track?

Step 5: Stay Flexible

Now, I know what you might be thinking. "But I have my self-care routine down already!" That is fantastic! However, life has a funny way of throwing curveballs at us when we least expect it. That is where staying flexible comes in. You might have your go-to strategies for managing stress or boosting your mood, when those strategies do not work anymore, that is when you need to be ready to switch things up. Experiment and try new things, maybe a different relaxation technique like deep breathing or progressive muscle relaxation. Or perhaps it is about being open to seeking support from friends, family, or a therapist when you need it most. Self-care is not a one-size-fits-all solution. What works for one person might not work for another, and that is perfectly okay. Stay open-minded and willing to adjust your approach as needed.

Step 6: Evaluate and Adjust for Your Self-Care Plan

Have you been putting in the work and practicing those self-care strategies we have been talking about? Now is the time to take a step back and evaluate how things are going. You know how it is with life and unexpected curveballs; that yoga routine you started is not quite doing the trick anymore, or perhaps those daily walks are not fitting into your schedule like they used to. That is totally okay. It is all part of the process. What is not part of the process, however, is you pretending not to notice those things.

So, here is what you do: take a moment to reflect. Ask yourself, "Are these self-care practices still serving me well?" Be honest with yourself. If something is not working anymore, it is time to adjust. You may need to switch up your routine, try something new, or even revisit some of the earlier steps we talked about. Do not be afraid to experiment until you find what truly nourishes your mind, body, and soul. So go ahead, evaluate, adjust, and keep on prioritizing your well-being. You've got this!

Step 7: Practice Self-Compassion for Your Self-Care Plan

A lot of us are too hard on ourselves, and we will not have that in self-care. To practice self-care, you need to treat yourself with kindness, understanding, and empathy, especially when you are going through a tough time or facing challenges. Give yourself permission to mess up and to still love yourself through it all. Practicing self-compassion is like flexing your muscles – it takes a bit of work, but the more you do it, the stronger it gets. Start by paying attention to your inner dialogue. Stop beating yourself up over every little mistake, and it is okay if you slip up. Nobody's perfect; when you catch yourself being hard on yourself, take a step back, take a deep breath, and remind yourself that you are human. Cut yourself some slack, acknowledge your humanity, embrace your imperfections, and love yourself anyway. Treat yourself with the same kindness, encouragement, and care that you would offer to a cherished friend. You deserve it, my friend.

Sleep Hygiene: Improving Sleep for Better Mental Health

Let us talk about something we all love but probably do not get enough of SLEEP. You must have heard "get a good night's sleep," before then most likely after hearing that, you go home and spend the night gaming or doing something else. Do you even know how important sleep is for your mental wellness?

Consistent lack of sleep can seriously mess with your mental health. You will be more irritable, forgetful, and just downright cranky. Chronic sleep deprivation has also been linked to anxiety, depression, and even more serious mental health issues. Elizabeth Blake Zakarin, a clinical psychologist and assistant professor of psychology, has proven this by saying that sleep deprivation can affect mental health. But fear not! There is still hope. You can start getting enough quality sleep. Sleeping well is like hitting the reset button for your brain. When you snooze, your brain gets a chance to repair and recharge, leaving you feeling refreshed and ready to tackle whatever life throws your way.

So, how can you ensure you're getting the sleep you need? Well, first off, make it a priority. I know Netflix binges and late-night scrolling sessions are tempting, but trust me, your brain will thank you for going to bed at a decent hour. If you are having trouble drifting off, establish a bedtime routine and create a comfortable sleep environment. Sleep is a necessity for good mental health, so tuck yourself in, turn off the lights, and get ready to snooze your way to a happier, healthier you. Sweet dreams!

Tips for Improving Sleep Hygiene

I know you would have probably heard a bunch of advice about getting better sleep before. It was still mentioned in the previous subtopic, wasn't it? However, let us look at it from the angle of the tips to improve your sleep hygiene.

1. Setting Up a Cozy Sleep Environment:

Your bedroom is your own personal sleep sanctuary. Keep it cool, dark, and quiet. Invest in some good curtains to block out light, and maybe even consider some earplugs or a white noise machine if you are easily disturbed by sounds.

2. Create Bedtime Routines:

Routines sound boring, but bedtime routines work wonders for your sleep. Wind down before bed with some relaxing activities like reading, taking a warm bath, or doing some gentle stretching. Also, always put your phone away at least an hour before bedtime; the blue light can mess with your body's natural sleep cycle.

3. Managing Stress and Worries:

You are lying in bed with your mind racing a mile a minute. Way out is jotting down your thoughts in a journal before going to bed. It helps clear your mind and ease those racing thoughts and if you are feeling really wound up, try some relaxation techniques like deep breathing or meditation to help calm your nerves.

4. Stick to a Sleep Schedule:

As tempting as it is to stay up late binge-watching your favorite show or scrolling through social media, please try to resist the urge. Stick to a sleep schedule and aim for a consistent bedtime and wake-up time every day, even on weekends – your body will thank you for it.

Addressing Common Sleep Disorders and Disturbances

Sleep disorders are conditions that affect the ability to sleep well on a regular basis. A sign of sleep disorder could be when you are lying in bed, tossing, and turning, unable to drift off into dreamland or you are constantly waking up throughout the night, feeling exhausted even after a full night's sleep. Sleep disorders can come in many shapes and forms.

Therefore, anything that messes with your ability to get the restorative sleep your body and mind needs to function at their best is a sleep disorder. Understanding these disorders can help you get the quality sleep you deserve. So, let us explore these sleep disturbances together and uncover what they are all about.

Insomnia

Contrary to what most people think, insomnia is not just about tossing and turning all night. It is about the frustration and exhaustion that comes from not being able to get the sleep you need. Imagine you are wide awake in the middle of the night staring at the ceiling, wondering why sleep seems to be playing hide and seek with you. That is insomnia; it affects millions of people worldwide and can be a real pain in the neck.

Fortunately, there are ways to combat insomnia and reclaim your nights of peaceful slumber. Good *sleep hygiene* can do the trick. As established in the previous subtopic, I am not talking about washing your sheets but about setting up a bedtime routine that tells your body, "Hey, it's time to sleep." You can also create a *cozy sleep environment*- comfy pillows, soft blankets, and a room that is just the right temperature. Say goodbye to screens at least an hour before bed. Instead, read a book, practice some gentle yoga, or indulge in a relaxing bath.

Lastly, fuel your body with a balanced diet, regular exercise, avoid caffeine and heavy meals close to bedtime. If you find yourself tossing and turning despite your best efforts, don't panic. Instead, try some relaxation techniques to help calm your mind. Deep breathing exercises, meditation, or progressive muscle relaxation can all help you into dreamland. If you are still struggling with insomnia after all this, reach out to your healthcare provider for guidance and support.

Snorers nemesis

Snorer's nemesis is a disruptor of peaceful slumber. You would have likely endured its relentless assault on your sleep. The culprit for this is snoring - the noisy orchestra of vibrations caused by the obstruction of airflow through the air passages during sleep. While it may seem harmless to the snorer, it can be a nuisance for their bedmate, robbing them of precious sleep and testing the limits of their sanity.

Do not worry; there are ways to combat it and reclaim your precious sleep.

First, you can change your sleeping position or encourage the snorer to sleep on their side rather than their back. This can help keep their airways open and reduce the intensity of snoring. Lifestyle changes like maintaining a healthy diet and incorporating regular exercise can work wonders since excess weight can exacerbate snoring.

Similarly, cutting back on alcohol and sedatives before bedtime can help relax the muscles in the throat and reduce the likelihood of snoring. For those seeking a more immediate solution, tap into the power of technology. Nasal strips, mouthpieces, and even specialized pillows are available to help keep air passages clear and minimize snoring.

Experiment with different options to find what works best for you and the snorer. When discussing the disorder, approach the subject with empathy and understanding. To be candid, snoring is beyond the snorer's control. They are asleep when it happens. So, work together to find solutions that benefit both parties and prioritize a good night's sleep for all involved.

Restless legs syndrome (RLS)

Restless legs syndrome is a condition where you feel this irresistible urge to move your legs, especially when you are trying to relax or sleep. It is like your legs just will not sit still, and trust me, it can be beyond frustrating!

Now, you might be thinking, "Just try to force them to stay still or something?" or you have probably thought of very creative ways of keeping the legs restrained. Sorry to burst your bubbles, but you are wrong. I know it sounds counterintuitive when your legs are already feeling restless, but sometimes, a little movement is all they need to calm down. So, take a short stroll around the room or do some gentle stretches to give those legs a break. Another trick is massage. Grab some lotion or oil, and give those restless limbs a good rubdown. Not only does it feel amazing, but it can also help relax the muscles and ease that urge to move. Also, try relaxation techniques and cut back on caffeine and alcohol, especially before bedtime. Things like deep breathing, meditation, or even soaking in a warm bath can also work wonders for calming both your mind and your legs. Restless legs syndrome might be a bit of a nuisance, but armed with these tips, you will be well-equipped to tackle it head-on.

Narcolepsy

Narcolepsy is a neurological disorder that affects the brain's ability to regulate sleep-wake cycles properly. People with narcolepsy experience sudden and uncontrollable episodes of falling asleep, even in the middle of activities like working, talking, or driving. Imagine feeling like you are about to sleep at any moment, regardless of what you are doing – that is narcolepsy for you.

Here are a few strategies to combat it:

1. Stick to a sleep schedule: Establish a consistent sleep routine to help regulate your body's internal clock and reduce the frequency of sudden sleep attacks. Aim for seven to nine hours of quality sleep each night, and try to go to bed and wake up at the same time every day – yes, even on weekends.

2. Nap strategically: While napping might seem like a no-brainer for someone with narcolepsy, it is essential to nap intentionally. Short, scheduled naps throughout the day can help manage daytime sleepiness without disrupting your nighttime sleep patterns.

3. Stay active: Regular physical activity can improve overall sleep quality and boost daytime alertness. Incorporate exercise into your daily routine and stick with it.

4.   Watch your diet: Certain foods and beverages can affect sleep quality and worsen narcolepsy symptoms. Limit your intake of caffeine and alcohol, especially close to bedtime, and opt for a balanced diet rich in fruits, vegetables, and whole grains.

5.   Seek support: Do not be afraid to reach out for help, whether it is from friends, family, or healthcare professionals. Having a support system in place can make a world of difference.

Narcolepsy might be a challenge, but with the right strategies, you can minimize its impact on your daily life and get back to doing what you love, fully awake and alert.

Sleepwalking

Sleepwalking happens when you are fast asleep, dreaming away, and suddenly your body decides it is time for a midnight stroll... except that you are still asleep! Sleepwalking, also known as somnambulism, is when someone walks or does other activities while they are still in a deep sleep state. It is like your body is on autopilot, wandering around without your conscious mind at the wheel.

Dealing with sleepwalking can be a bit tricky, but safety first. If you or someone you know is prone to sleepwalking, make sure the sleepwalker's environment is safe and secure by removing any potential hazards, like sharp objects or obstacles that could cause tripping. Also, improve your sleep habits to help reduce the frequency of sleepwalking episodes, but if sleepwalking becomes persistent, seek professional help. A visit to a sleep specialist or doctor can provide valuable ideas and potential solutions tailored to your specific situation. Sleepwalking might seem strange or even a bit scary (except you are not scared of midnight trips taken unconsciously), but with the right approach, you can take control and get a good night's sleep without any midnight wanderings.

In this chapter, we delved into the crucial elements of mental wellness through the exploration of self-care practices and sleep hygiene. We highlighted the impact that self-care has on mental well-being and emphasized the importance of nurturing the mind, body, and soul through various activities and strategies. We have also gone through the process of creating a personalized self-care plan and prioritizing self-care. We established that individuals can enhance their physical, emotional, and spiritual well-being to reduce stress and boost overall wellness. Furthermore, we discussed the significance of quality sleep for maintaining mental health. We discussed its role in restoring and recharging the brain. There were also tips for improving sleep hygiene, addressing common sleep disorders and disturbances, and offering strategies to combat them.

In the next chapter, we will be discussing technology and digital detox for mental well-being through the lens of the impact of tech on mental health, promoting healthy tech habits, and the benefits of digital detox.

Chapter 8

Technology and Digital Detox for Mental Well-being

It is no secret that technology has become an integral part of our daily lives. From smartphones to social media platforms, we are constantly bombarded with notifications, updates, and information overload. While technology has undoubtedly brought about numerous benefits and conveniences, it has also raised concerns about its impact on our mental well-being.

Impact Of Tech on Mental Well-Being

Let us talk about how tech is messing with our heads. You have probably heard a ton about it already, right? After all, people make videos about how technology is affecting us using technology and, of course, post them on platforms made using technology. Genius, right? You see, we are constantly bombarded with stuff about screen time, social media, and how our gadgets are wrecking our mental well-being, but let us get real for a second: do we really get how deep this goes? Sure, we might think we do, but there is always more.

Tech has totally transformed how we live, work, and connect with each other. It has made life easier in so many ways, but it also comes with some serious problems, especially when it comes to our mental health.

Social media, for instance, is like a love-hate relationship. On one hand, it is awesome for keeping up with friends, sharing memes, and feeling like you are part of a global community. However, it can mess with your head, too. The pressure to keep up appearances, rack up likes, and present this picture-perfect life is exhausting. Let us not even get started on the fear of missing out when you see everyone else living their best lives while you are just chilling in your PJs.

And then there is screen time. Seriously, many of us have our eyeballs glued to screens 24/7, whether for work, binge-watching Netflix, or mindlessly scrolling through TikTok; we just can not seem to tear ourselves away. Unfortunately, all that screen time is wreaking havoc on our sleep, our stress levels, and our overall sanity. In fact, according to a BBC article, Dr. George Kitsaras says that screens can affect your sleep patterns before bed. Ever find yourself lying in bed at 3 AM, mind buzzing with notifications and memes? That is the effect of all that screen time.

Pardon me for dwelling too much on the bad news, but it is not all bad news. Tech has some tricks for boosting our mental health, too. Meditation apps, online therapy, you name it. There are tons of tools out there to help us chill out, de-stress, and find peace in this crazy digital world. So, I am not just a bearer of bad news. There is good news, too.

Promoting Healthy Tech Habits

Have you ever stopped to think about how much time you spend glued to your screens each day? We're talking about smartphones, tablets, laptops – you name it. Those little routines we have developed around our gadgets and screens are our tech habits. Though our devices connect us to the world, keep us entertained, and help us stay organized, we need to use them in moderation. Now, I know what you are probably thinking. "But I need my phone for work, for staying in touch with friends, for everything!" Well, Dr. Maurice G. Sholas, a pediatric physical rehabilitation physician in New Orleans, agrees with you. She said, "Screen time is like sugar. You shouldn't cut it all the way out because there is a need and a purpose for it." I know our tech is pretty much ingrained into every aspect of our lives. But just like every other thing, it is all about finding a balance.

That brings us to the question: How much screen time can start to take a toll on our well-being?

The answer to that is that healthy tech is different for everyone. Nonetheless, I will be taking you through some ideas to get you started. First, give yourself some tech-free zones or times during the day. You can put your phone away during meals or ban screens from the bedroom before bedtime. Also, anytime you find yourself scrolling mindlessly through social media for hours on end, try setting a timer to remind yourself to take a break every now and then. Get up, stretch, go for a walk – anything to give your eyes and brain a rest.

Additionally, before you reach for your phone out of habit, ask yourself why you are doing it. Being more mindful about your tech usage can help you break free from those automatic habits. Prioritize your connection with people because texting and messaging can be convenient, but nothing beats face-to-face interaction. So, make an effort to spend quality time with friends and family without being distracted by screens. Lastly, just like you brush your teeth every day, make it a habit to tidy up your digital life, too. Delete those unused apps, organize your files, and unsubscribe from those emails and newsletters you never read. Promoting healthy tech habits does not have to be rocket science. It is all about finding that balance that works for you.

Digital Detox

Imagine a day without the constant ping of notifications, without the urge to check your socials every five minutes– that's a digital detox. Digital detox is all about reclaiming your time, your focus, and your sanity. It is about stepping back from digital devices and reconnecting with the real world.

The secret of digital detox is to provide a chance to recharge your mental batteries and rediscover the simple joys of life offline. I know it might feel weird at first going through withdrawal from your digital reliance, but once you break free from the digital grip, you will feel lighter, clearer, and more present than ever before.

So, why not give it a try? Take a day, a weekend, or even a whole week if you are feeling brave. Put down the phone, step away from the screen, and see what happens. Who knows, you might just find a whole new world waiting for you beyond the digital.

Benefits of Digital Detox

The benefits of a digital detox are numerous, but we will just be looking at a few in this book. I don't want to bore you, after all.

Reduced Stress

When you are constantly bombarded with emails, notifications, and social media updates, you are likely to have your stress level skyrocket. Taking a break from your digital devices can actually help alleviate that stress. By disconnecting from the virtual world, you give your mind a chance to unwind and reset. This leads to a calmer state of being.

Improved Sleep

The struggle of scrolling through your phone late into the night, only to regret it when your alarm goes off in the morning, should be familiar. Well, here is the scoop: the blue light emitted by screens can mess with your sleep cycle, making it harder to fall asleep and stay asleep. But fear not! A digital detox before bedtime can help regulate your sleep patterns, leading to better sleep quality and overall well-being.

Enhanced Productivity

It may sound counterintuitive, but taking time away from your devices can actually make you more productive. Think about the number of times you have been in the middle of a task only to be derailed by a notification or social media update. By detoxing from digital distractions, you can focus better on the task at hand and get more done in less time.

Better Relationship

Ever been out with friends or family, only to find everyone glued to their phones? Maybe you have even been one of those glued to their devices one or two times? Constant digital distraction can hinder meaningful face-to-face interactions. By taking a break from your devices, you can fully engage with the people around you, strengthening relationships and fostering deeper connections.

Increased Mindfulness

In today's hyper-connected world, it is easy to lose touch with the present moment. However, by stepping away from your devices, you can cultivate mindfulness and fully immerse yourself in the here and now. Whether taking a walk in nature or simply enjoying a meal without distractions, a digital detox allows you to experience life in real-time, free from the confines of screens and notifications.

Enhanced Mental Wellbeing

Excessive screen time has been linked to increased stress,

anxiety, and depression. Taking a break from technology can give your mind a much-needed respite from the constant barrage of information and stimulation. This will allow you to recharge and rejuvenate your mental health by restoring balance and tranquility to your mind.

Foster Creativity

Constant exposure to digital content can stifle your creativity and imagination by inundating your mind with pre-packaged ideas and information. I mean, why think of hacks and ways to get things done faster when you can just watch a video on it on "10-minute Craft"?

By disconnecting from screens, you can create space for your creativity to flourish. You allow your mind to wander, explore, and generate new ideas. It can be through writing, drawing, painting, or experimenting with a new hobby. A digital detox can help unlock your creative potential and inspire you to think outside the box.

Promotes Physical Activity

Spending too much time sitting in front of screens can take a toll on your physical health and well-being. A digital detox can encourage you to get moving and engage in physical activities that nourish your body and soul.

Improves Attention Span

The constant multitasking and rapid information processing required by digital devices can train your brain to seek out constant stimulation and instant gratification. A break from screens can make your brain focus for longer periods of time, therefore improving your attention span and concentration. It also helps sharpen your cognitive skills and enhance your ability to engage deeply with the world around you.

Cultivates a Sense of Balance

Finding a healthy balance between technology use and real-life experiences can be challenging. A digital detox can help you recalibrate your relationship with technology and rediscover a sense of balance in your life. Set boundaries around your digital usage, prioritize activities that nourish your mind, body, and spirit, and be intentional about how you engage with technology to create a more harmonious and fulfilling life that honors both your digital and offline experiences.

In this chapter, we discussed the challenges and opportunities technology has on our mental well-being and how promoting healthy tech habits is key to finding balance in our increasingly digital lives. We also went ahead to encourage embracing digital detox to reclaim control over our time, focus, and overall sanity by stating the vast benefits digital detox has on various aspects of our well-being. With this, we can cultivate a more fulfilling and balanced lifestyle that honors both our digital and offline worlds. In the next chapter, we will talk about the three major life transitions, the coping strategies for navigating these changes, how to manage grief and loss through support, and building resilience in the face of adversity.

Chapter 9

Overcoming Major Life Transitions

Divorce, Loss, and Career Changes

Navigating major life transitions like divorce, loss, or career changes can feel like walking through an unknown territory. You may think you have it all figured out, but when faced with the confusion of significant transitions, you can be left feeling disoriented. In this chapter, we will explore what these transitions entail and how we can overcome them.

Divorce

Divorce is one of those life transitions that many of us have heard about so often that it almost feels like we could navigate through it with our eyes closed. However, is that really true?

At its core, divorce marks the end of a significant chapter in our lives. It is not just about legally dissolving a marriage; it is about untangling emotions, rearranging priorities, and redefining identities. It is a journey through a series of emotions, from grief and anger to relief and acceptance. Just when you think you have processed it all, there is another wave of emotions waiting to crash over you. Nevertheless, amidst the pain and uncertainty, there lies an opportunity for growth and renewal.

Overcoming divorce is not just about surviving it but more about thriving despite it. It involves finding the strength to pick up the pieces, creating a new beginning, rediscovering who you are outside of the confines of a relationship, and embracing the opportunities that lie ahead.

Going through a divorce requires embracing the process of healing, seeking support from loved ones, patience, resilience, and a whole lot of self-love. Reclaim your independence, pursue your passions, and emerge from divorce stronger and more resilient than ever before to build the life you have always dreamed of.

Loss

Loss is all about losing something or someone you hold dear. Who or what it may be is gone suddenly, and your world will definitely change drastically. Loss is not just confined to the realm of relationships. You may pour your heart and soul into a job, maybe even build your identity around it, only to have it ripped away from you. Suddenly, you are adrift, wondering who you are without that job title and a sense of purpose.

There is also the loss of loved ones, whether through death or distance. It is a gut-wrenching ache that never quite goes away, no matter how much time passes. You find yourself reaching for the phone to call them, only to remember they are no longer there to answer. It is okay to feel lost, to grieve, to stumble along the way. However, pause for a moment and find the strength within yourself to keep moving forward and carve out a new path even when the old one has crumbled beneath your feet.

Career changes

Career changes, whether by choice or circumstance, can be both exhilarating and daunting. Imagine you have been cruising along at your job for years, maybe even decades, and suddenly everything has changed; you lost your job, or maybe you simply feel that it is time for something new. Just like we have been peeling off the layers of stress and mental health, changing your professional path is more than just updating your resume or scrolling through job listings. It encompasses embracing uncertainty, redefining your goals, and charting a new course.

At this stage, feeling apprehensive is natural because change is never easy, especially when it comes to something as central to our lives as our careers. However, just as we scale through divorce or loss, this career transition stage will pass. Step back, reassess, and, most importantly, embrace the journey ahead with resilience and strength to overcome any obstacle that comes your way.

Coping Strategies for Navigating Major Life Changes

Now, how do we overcome these major life transitions that threaten to engulf us? An array of coping strategies is available to find your way through all the challenges associated with major life changes. Let us go through some of it together.

Change is inevitable, and it is okay to feel overwhelmed, anxious, or even excited about major life changes.

Acknowledging these emotions will give you the opportunity to experience them without judgment. Embrace the idea that change is a natural part of life and diffuse the anxiety that accompanies the change into thin air. One tried-and-true coping strategy is to lean on your support network. Lean on family, friends, or a trusted mentor during times of transition. Feel free to reach out and lean on those who care about you. Having someone to talk to can provide much-needed perspective and emotional support.

Another helpful tactic is to focus on what you can control. While you may not be able to control the circumstances of change, you can control how you respond to them. Take stock of your strengths and resources, and channel your energy into making positive choices that align with your goals and values. For example, if you lose your job, you can take stock of the skills and possible references you have and even decide to spend more time on LinkedIn.

Next, remember to give yourself some grace. It is okay to feel overwhelmed or uncertain during times of change. Take a deep breath, cut yourself some slack, and remind yourself that it is okay not to have all the answers right away. So, anytime you see that job postings need more years of experience than what you have or realize that no other relative can do what the one you lost used to do, do not break down.

While at it, don't forget to practice self-care along the way. Take care of your physical, emotional, and mental well-being during these times by engaging in activities that bring you joy and nourish your soul. Change is constant, so be patient with yourself as you navigate the twists and turns of life. Celebrate your victories, no matter how small, and trust that with time, you will emerge from this period of change stronger and more resilient than ever before.

Grief and Loss: Processing Emotions and Finding Support

Grief is that deep, heavy feeling that settles in your chest when you lose someone or something dear to you. It is not just about sadness. It is a whole spectrum of emotions — talk of anger, guilt, confusion, even relief. Dealing with emotions and memories and adjusting to a new reality without someone or something we cherish can be messy and unpredictable, and it does not follow a set timeline, so if you are feeling all over the place, you are not alone. It is okay to feel all those things. In fact, all the emotions are necessary.

The specific way to process emotions and find support in times of grief and loss differs from person to person, so you won't be seeing a step-by-step process here. However, here is the basics. For starters, do not push those emotions away while going through grief; do not rush or ignore it; rather, face them head-on. Allow yourself to feel the full range of emotions that come with the loss, whether it is sadness, anger, confusion, or even relief, and then find healthy ways to cope with them.

Passing through grief alone is overwhelming. You, therefore, need to find support from friends, family, support groups, or therapy. Relating with people who understand what you are going through can make all the difference. They will listen without judgment, understand your pain, and help you scale through the darkest moments in your life. Amidst grief, do not be hard on yourself; it is perfectly fine if you do not have it all together; take your time to heal and find peace amidst the pain.

Building Resilience in The Face of Adversity

Has life been throwing curveballs your way lately? Maybe it is a tough breakup, a job loss, or even just the everyday stresses that seem to pile up. Do not let that deter you from forging ahead. We all face adversity at some point, but how we bounce back from it builds our resilience.

Resilience goes beyond being tough and putting on a brave face. It is your ability to adapt and grow stronger in the face of adversity. The more you work on building resilience, the stronger you get. Adversity comes in different forms; it ranges from major life crises to everyday challenges. It could be losing a loved one, facing financial struggles, or dealing with health issues, and it could also be as simple as a bad day at work or an argument with a friend. No matter the form it comes in, each challenge presents an opportunity for growth.

So, how do we build resilience? In the same way, sturdy buildings are constructed with commitment and investment. Let us break it down together. First, change your mindset, see challenges as opportunities for growth instead of crumbling under pressure, and see setbacks as temporary roadblocks and not a dead end. So, start by shifting your perspective; those obstacles are chances to learn and improve.

Next is self-care; resilience cannot be built on its own. You need to take care of yourself while you are at it. Prioritize your needs and make yourself happy. A trip to Malibu? Go for it! It is part of your resilience-building journey.

Also, practice makes perfect; build your resilience like you build any other skill. It takes time and effort, but do not get discouraged if you stumble along the way. Every setback is just another opportunity to flex and come back even stronger. Finally, do not stay stuck in the same old patterns. Embrace change and find new ways to thrive. Be flexible and adaptable; instead of fearing change, embrace it as an opportunity for growth.

In this chapter, we discussed managing major life transitions with emphasis on divorce, loss, and career changes, then we highlighted some coping mechanisms to overcome these life challenges, like acknowledging our emotions, leaning on our support network, and focusing on what we can control. Afterward, we shed light on managing the emotions associated with grief and loss by facing it head-on through support from loved ones or therapy. We also discussed building resilience. In the next chapter, we will be discussing how to normalize mental health conversations.

Chapter 10

Normalizing Mental Health Conversations

Think about it for a second. How often do you catch yourself saying, "I'm fine" when someone asks how you are doing? And how often do you really mean it? Exactly. We have become professionals at brushing off our struggles like they are no big deal. But guess what? They are a big deal. This is where normalizing mental health conversations comes in.

Normalizing mental health conversations is not about plastering a fake smile on your face and pretending everything is going well. Nope, it is about ripping off that mask and showing the world the real you – flaws and all. It is about opening up, being vulnerable, and letting others know that it is okay not to be okay.

Sure, it might feel awkward at first. I mean, we have been conditioned to keep our struggles locked up tight, right? But here is the thing: the more we talk about mental health, the less power it has over us. Because guess what? You are not alone. We are all in this crazy ride called life.

So next time someone asks how you are doing, don't just settle for "I'm fine." Open up, share your struggles, and watch as the walls come tumbling down. When we normalize mental health conversations, we create a world where everyone feels seen, heard, and understood. And trust me, that is a world worth fighting for.

That is a lot of discussion about normalizing mental health discussions. However, how do we go about it? We can start by addressing the Stigma and misconception and encouraging open dialogue.

Stigma and Misconception Surrounding Mental Health

Stigma is like this cloud hanging over mental health, making people hesitant to talk about it openly. Misconceptions? Well, they are the myths and misunderstandings that fuel that stigma. So, if people believe that people living with psychosis become serial killers, that is a misconception. However, if this prevents people living with psychosis from speaking about their condition, then it has become a stigma. There are many forms stigma and misconception can take. Let us look at a few and see if we are guilty of those.

1.   **The Blame Game:** One common misconception is the idea that mental health struggles are just a matter of personal weakness or lack of character. Some people even think it is a punishment for bad behavior or that people with mental health disorders were just not raised well or are not strong enough. However, mental health issues do not discriminate. They can affect anyone, regardless of their strength or willpower. It is not about pointing fingers. It is about understanding and support.

2. **The Mask Effect:** Ever heard of the phrase "putting on a brave face"? Many individuals struggling with mental health challenges often feel pressured to hide their struggles behind a facade of normalcy. However, pretending everything is okay only increases the stigma and prevents open conversations about mental health.

3. **The Myth of Perfection**: Society often glorifies the idea of perfection, painting a picture of flawless lives without room for struggles. This unrealistic standard creates a breeding ground for stigma, making it hard for people to speak up about their mental health concerns for fear of judgment. In this situation, people with mental health disorders think they are flawed, so they keep this flaw under wraps.

4. **Improper Use of Language:** Words hold a lot of power, and our use of language can either perpetuate stigma or promote understanding. Terms like "crazy," "psycho," or "nuts" increase the stigma against mental health issues.

Encouraging Open Dialogue and Seeking Support

People use the phrase "it's okay not to be okay" often, but do we truly embrace it? Sometimes, we need to talk about what is going on inside our heads, whether it is anxiety, depression, or just feeling overwhelmed. Opening up can be tough, I get it, but trust me, sharing your struggles with someone you trust can be a game-changer. It could be a friend, a family member, or a professional therapist – whoever makes you feel comfortable. And hey, it is not just about talking; it is about actively listening too. If someone reaches out to you, be there for them. Offer a listening ear, a shoulder to lean on, or simply a reassuring hug. Let them know they are not alone in this journey.

So, how do you do that?

1.   **Open Dialogue**: First things first, let us talk. We are not just talking about small talk here; we are talking about real, meaningful conversations about how we are feeling. It is about creating a space where people feel comfortable about opening up about their struggles without fear of judgment or stigma. Whether it is with friends, family, or a professional, opening up can be the first step towards healing.

2.   **Breaking the Silence:** Mental health is not something to be whispered about behind closed doors. By sharing our own experiences and listening to others, we can chip away at the stigma surrounding mental health and create a more supportive community for everyone.

3.   **Seeking Support:** No one should have to go through tough times alone. Whether you are dealing with stress, anxiety, depression, or any other mental health challenge, it is crucial to reach out for support. Whether it is talking to a

therapist, joining a support group, or confiding in a trusted friend, seeking help is a sign of strength, not weakness.

4.   **Exploring Resources:** Thankfully, there is a wealth of resources available for those in need. From online forums and helplines to therapy apps and community organizations, there's something out there for everyone. Don't be afraid to explore your options and find the support that works best for you.

So, let us keep the mental health conversation going. Let us continue to encourage open dialogue, break the silence surrounding mental health, and support each other on our journey towards better mental well-being. Remember, you're not alone, and help is always within reach.

In this chapter, we discussed how we can normalize having mental health conversations. We looked at how to address stigma and misconception and encourage open discussion.

Conclusion

We have come to the end of this book, and it suddenly feels like I am losing my travel companions after traveling the world with them. It is fine; I am just being dramatic. I know you probably didn't travel beyond your couch while reading this book.

In the introduction of this book, it was mentioned that we live in a world where many of us chase time, and we just keep wishing we had more time. Unfortunately, there is no extra time, and chasing time can cause stress, which is detrimental to our mental health. So, instead of chasing time, let us divert the little time we have from the stressors to the things that give us peace. DO YOU?!

This entire book and the way to achieve mental wellness and deal with mental stress can be summarized in just 2 sentences– "Do you!" and "You come first." Every single tip, coping mechanism, and practical technique falls under that. So, even if you cannot follow every tip in this book, always remember to do it and put yourself first.

Bibliography

American Psychological Association (2023, March 8). Stress Effects On The Body. *APA*. https://www.apa.org/topics/stress/body

Bob Fanelli. (2021, April 25). Healing the hurt: hips. *bobfanelli*. https://www.bobfanelli.com/post/healing-the-hurt-hips

CNBC. (2023, April 11). Your Money: 70% Of Americans Are Feeling Financially Stressed, New Cnbc Survey Finds. *CNBC* https://www.cnbc.com/2023/04/11/70percent-of-americans-feel-financially-stressed-new-cnbc-survey-finds.html#:~:text=As%20a%20group%2C%20women%20are%20feeling%20more,to%20paycheck%20and%20have%20no%20emergency%20savings

Couric, K. (2021, May 25). Dr. Herbert Benson on Sleep and the Mind-Body Connection. *Katie Couric Media*. https://katiecouric.com/health/2245-2/

Cuda, G. (2010, December 6). Just Breathe: Body has a Built-In Stress Reliever. *NPR*. https://www.npr.org/2010/12/06/131734718/just-breathe-body-has-a-built-in-stress-reliever#:~:text=Changing%20Gene%20Expression,alter%20the%20body's%20stress%20response.

De Oliveira, C., Saka, M., Bone, L. *et al.* The Role of Mental Health on Workplace Productivity: A Critical Review of the Literature. *Appl Health Econ Health Policy* **21**, 167–193 (2023). https://doi.org/10.1007/s40258-022-00761-w

Dusang, K. (2019, May 9). How Stress Can Affect Your Sleep. *Baylor*

College of Medicine. https://www.bcm.edu/news/how-stress-can-affect-your-sleep

Errera, R. (2023, August 24). Eye-Opening Work-Life Balance Statistics. *Toner Buzz.* Retrieved from https://www.tonerbuzz.com/blog/worklife-balance-statistics/

Felman, A. (2024, March 22). What is Mental Health? https://www.medicalnewstoday.com/articles/154543

Graber, E. (2022, January 11). Nutrition and Stress: a two-way street. *American Society for Nutrition.* https://nutrition.org/nutrition-and-stress-a-two-way-street/

Hampton, J. (2022, August 18). Report: 80% of Global Workers Experience Information Overload. *Datanami.* https://www.datanami.com/2022/08/18/report-80-of-global-workers-experience-information-overload/

Harvard Health. (2020, July 6). Understanding The Stress Response. https://www.health.harvard.edu/staying-healthy/understanding-the-stress-response

McLean Hospital (2023, November 20).Stress: What you need to know. https://www.mcleanhospital.org/essential/stress

Mindful awareness. (2024, January 8). Mindful Wellness Assessment. *University at Buffalo.* https://ed.buffalo.edu/mindful-assessment/scale/domains/mindful-awareness.html

MPR News. (2017, June 2). Emotional Health Key To Physical Health. *MPR News.* https://www.mprnews.org/story/2017/06/02/dr-vivek-murthy-on-emotional-health

Murray, W. (2022, February 8). Men Report More Relationship-Based

Mental Health Concerns. *Thriveworks.*
https://thriveworks.com/blog/research-widespread-
relationship-
anxiety/#:~:text=Men%20Report%20More%20Relationship-
Based,%25)%20than%20women%20(29%25)

Paul Hamlyn Foundation. (2014, December 18). Right Here: How To Commission Better Mental Health And Wellbeing Services For Young People. *Paul Hamlyn Foundation* https://www.phf.org.uk/reader/commission-better-mental-health-wellbeing-services-young-people/mean-mental-wellbeing/

Rapaport, L. (2024, January 19). Mood Swings: Definition, Causes, And How To Manage Them. *EverydayHealth.com.* https://www.everydayhealth.com/emotional-health/how-manage-mood-swings-naturally/

Shafer, E. (2020, May 21). Variety. *Variety.* https://variety.com/2020/music/news/lady-gaga-mental-health-mentorship-making-chromatica-interview-zane-lowe-1234612226/

Stanford University. (2016, April 9). Embracing Stress Is More Important Than Reducing Stress, Stanford Psychologist Says. *Stanford News.* https://news.stanford.edu/2015/05/07/stress-embrace-mcgonigal-050715/

WHO (2022, June 17). Mental health. *WHO* https://www.who.int/news-room/fact-sheets/detail/mental-health-strengthening-our-response

www.ingramcontent.com/pod-product-compliance
Lightning Source LLC
La Vergne TN
LVHW051750080426
835511LV00018B/3291